IS THERE A CURE FOR GRIEF?

NAVIGATING THE WORST PART OF LIFE

CAMARA WATKINS

AMARO GROUP
PUBLISHING

Mt Pleasant, SC

www.AmaroGroupServices.com

Cover Photo by André Watkins, Available at SoulinFocus.net

Paperback ISBN: 979-8-9853895-9-3

TABLE OF CONTENTS

DEDICATION

To my son:

I'm sorry you'll never hear her voice, so I sing loudly to you in perfect pitch every day.

I'm sorry you'll never taste her cooking, so I make you her peach cobbler and mac n cheese, with *All* the butter.

I'm sorry you'll never experience her unconditional love, so I accept you fully and stare daggers of love at you every chance I get.

I'm sorry you'll never know her high standards, so I teach you "The King's English" and lessons from the Book of Manners.

I'm sorry you won't know her, so I let her live on in you through your name.

I'm sorry you won't see her brilliant smile light up an entire room, so I show you your dimples and your eyes that came from her.

I'm sorry you won't feel her, so I moved to be close to your aunt and my aunt, who both remind me of her in all the best ways.

I'm sorry you won't know her commitment to diversity and inclusion, so I read you stories from various cultures and teach you to embrace difference.

I'm sorry you won't get to go to Leoni to celebrate Kwanzaa with our whole village, so I learned from her book and notes, and we'll celebrate with our family.

I'm sorry you know this version of me, so I am committed to being more than I am, so you have the best, like I did.

I love you. Like an action word.

WHY THIS BOOK?

Well, there's a reason you picked up this book. And for that, I give you my sincerest apologies. I know that loss is a part of life, but I am sorry that you and your loved one have gone through something that this book could be seen as a resource.

My life-altering loss was that of my Mother, and that turned my whole world upside down. She was the center of my universe, my dearest and closest friend, my confidant, the giver of my life, the most creative and giving person I've ever met, the "typest A" of type A personalities, the woman behind the saying that "a strong woman is like tea—you never know how strong she is until you put her in hot water", the quintessential problem-solver, the perfect mix of giving all the love while enforcing some pretty strict rules, and so much more. Losing her came as a shock; she did have cancer for 10 years but she'd weathered 2 Whipple surgeries, having to take a leave from work, going back to work, a liver transplant, going back to work again, a hospitalization, being put in hospice, and in that last month, regaining her strength and no longer qualifying for hospice care. I'd taken a leave from work to help care for her, but when she got better, I'd returned to my home. Next thing I knew, my dad was FaceTiming me to prove to me that she was gone. I totally loved my mother above all else, but I didn't really understand exactly how completely and fully she was the glue to my life and to that of my family (e.g., my sister, her husband/my father, her mother, her sister, her best friend/my godmother, her friends who care about my sister and me). As time has gone on, we've all had our various reactions, and the timelines for each of us have been different, and that has expanded my understanding of grief as well. All that to say, out of my discombobulation and excruciating pain, this book was born.

PREFACE 2

FOUR YEARS LATER

I wrote this book during the year following the loss of my mother. Four years later, the acuteness of this loss is still palpable, and I still cry hot, angry, grief-stricken tears when I need to. But my filter has mostly returned, and I am less pointed in my interactions with others. More pointed than I used to be, but less than I was in this book. In re-reading this book, I am struck by how the words reflect things I did not know were in me, and I'm tempted to keep this book to myself for fear of being mischaracterized or, worse, not helpful to whomever reads this book hoping to find relief. However, I wrote this as a guide for others to be helped when loss strikes and as an attempt to keep others from being hurt by those who care. The delivery may be offensive, but I ask that the packaging be educational for you to see this picture of acute grief and not a deterrent to hearing the messages.

A year after my mother passed, my maternal grandmother passed unexpectedly. She was a very active woman who had a busy schedule of work and volunteering up until the day she was rushed to the hospital. It was important to me to read this book in the wake of that loss as well and to see if the lessons still ring true. They do! It did illuminate for me differences in how I dealt with the loss and what I expected of others, but the tips are still applicable.

INTRODUCTION

It's time to stop consuming

and start creating.

Don't consume. Create!

I've finally made it back to the beach. It's a perfect day—sounds of the gentlest of waves aligning with my breathing. The sun is beaming down, but its harshest rays are blocked by my umbrella. There are not many people on this end of the beach. So, I'm feeling like I'm in an oasis amidst the Spring Break crowd. An oasis amidst my reality. And just like that, any time I truly think, my thoughts turn dark because (my) reality is dark. Yes, some choose to only think about the positive and we are taught that those are the good people, the goal. But isn't living in denial dangerous? Isn't it actually bad for your health? Isn't it a form of delusion?

So why am I forced to hide my darkness? Why am I forced to only interact when I can push my cheek muscles upward to resemble a smile and nod politely while others talk about meaningless shit and babble endlessly about all that is good, when all is not?

If you picked this book up hoping to get a happy ending, I'm sorry to disappoint you because that is not what happened. Spoiler alert, my mom did not pull a "Jesus" resurrection on me—though

1

admittedly, my fingers are still crossed for that one. I don't think a happy ending is possible, and I may even be mad if the Disney-loving side of me takes over and tries to wrap this up in a neat bow. Guess we'll see.

Tips to help you get through this book:

A. I love lists. My mind automatically organizes things into lists and tries to create order.

B. My mind, post-grief, veers into multiple directions and finds it hard to stick to a particular list or structure or sense of time, even. However, I think it's important for you to see that and not have it edited out. So some lists start but may stop or may not continue following a perfect APA style. Trust me, I'm Columbia-educated and could make it work if I wanted. But try and follow the imperfect flow of a grief-ridden mind with something important to tell you. That's way more important than list structure.

That said…

Tip 3. This book doesn't have to be read in order. I gave you the preface so you know what I went through and to share some of the magnificence of who she was. I don't have it in me to fully write her story in the way she deserves, but it seemed like giving some kind of summary would be helpful after some of the harsher shit I said… But feel free to jump to where you think would be most helpful or most interesting.

Warning/Maybe Tip 4: I will hurt your feelings in one way or another. I don't *want* to, but I am choosing to be honest by sharing my real thoughts and emotions. I want to help you gain insight into the grief experience. My goal is not to be hurtful, but I choose not to edit (all) the hurt out. Hopefully you will keep reading because I don't want you to miss the good stuff due to the ugly packaging. But if it's too much for you, do what's best for you. I totally understand.

PART A

A RUDE AWAKENING

I re-watched the movie 'The Matrix' the other day. I didn't just stumble upon it or anything like that. I decided to watch the movie again because Keanu Reeves had been on one of the daytime talk shows promoting a new movie, and they remarked how it had been 20 years since the release of 'The Matrix.' It sounded unreal to know that I've been alive long enough to have seen that movie and still remember it so vividly. But alas, here we are. That remark about the movie prompted me to check our streaming services a few evenings later, and lo & behold, 'The Matrix' was on one. Spoiler Alert. If you haven't seen it, stop reading and go watch it. It's an awesome movie. Totally revolutionary, and there is still nothing quite like it.

So while re-watching, I realized I did not really remember the main plot of the movie. I only remembered the characters and the fighting scenes, which I'm still really into. But the central premise is something I now can't get out of my head. I think we've all been told a lie since our births to keep us in line. They do this so we don't freak out and have crises of identity and/or care about things we possibly can't do anything about. In this movie, there's The One, who is able to break their bondage of ignorance and actual servitude, and in real life, I remember my parents discussing the movie with their friends and all the church folk. They talked about the metaphor of Neo (The One) being Jesus (also known as The One) who saves. However, therein lies the fantasy we're all living. The lie to keep us happy in our incubators.

And yet, that doesn't/isn't even working. So what's the point of that? I believe that we all need something to live for—a reason, some hope, something to fight or work towards. And without that, we flounder horribly. So, we created higher powers, higher callings, something bigger and more powerful than ourselves that we can't see or fully explain because that both feels more majestic and—well—powerful/bigger than us and also can't be explained.

When I adhered to these beliefs myself, I would have read the previous paragraphs and felt profound sadness for their writer. I would have felt sorrow that they had not experienced the love of God that I had, the joy of hope, and the peace of understanding, and I would have assumed their perspective came from ignorance. But let me assure you, my perspective comes from knowing too much.

CHAPTER 1

LOSING FAITH

HOPE

Intransitive verb

To cherish a desire with anticipation, to want something to happen or be true

// hopes for a promotion

// hoping for the best

// hope so

archaic: Trust

Transitive verb

1. To desire with expectation of obtainment or fulfillment

// hope she remembers

// hopes to be invited

2. To expect with confidence, trust

// your mother is doing well, I hope

Hope against hope: to hope without any basis for expecting fulfillment

Noun

1. archaic: trust, reliance

2. *a*: a desire accomplished by expectation of or belief in fulfillment

// came in hopes of seeing you

also: expectation of fulfillment or success

// no hope for a cure

// when they were young and full of hope

b: someone or something on which hopes are centered

// our only hope for victory

c: something desired or hoped for

// great hopes for the coming year

EXPECT

Intransitive verb

1. archaic: wait, stay

2. to look forward

3. to be pregnant, await the birth of one's child

Transitive verb

1. archaic: await

2. to anticipate or look forward to the coming or occurrence of

// we expect them any minute now

// expected a phone call

    1. suppose, think

    2. a: to consider probable or certain

// expect to be forgiven

// expect that things will improve

    b: to consider reasonable, due or necessary

// expected hard work from the student

    c: to consider bound in duty or obligated

    // they expect you to pay your bills

Expect, hope - both mean to await some occurrence or outcome

Expect implies a high degree of certainty and usually involves the idea of preparing or envisioning // expects to be finished by Tuesday

Hope implies little certainty but suggests confidence or assurance in the possibility that what one desires or longs for will happen // hope to find work soon

End of Merriam-Webster notations

I could choose the form of hope that does not involve expectation, but if faith/God is involved, then that is not biblical.

Faith is something hoped for, evidence of things not seen (Hebrews 11:1). We are required to have faith to believe not only in God but also in His promises. He promises healing (Isaiah 53:5, Psalm 147:3, James 5:14-15), strength (Isaiah 41:10, Philippians 4:13), to move mountains (Mark 11:23-24), to answer if you call (Jeremiah 33:3, Isaiah 65:24), to give better than you could have asked for (Matthew 7:11). The caveat is that He always has an out. Read all of Psalm 34 for this incredible juxtaposition of promises and caveats. It can't be that He doesn't exist; rather, you must not have even had mustard seed faith, or you had some doubt (Matthew 17:20, Mark 11:23) or you must not be righteous because the prayers of the righteous availeth much (James 5:16) or you weren't humble or must be wicked (2 Chronicles 7:14). It forces you to try and eliminate the natural human emotion of doubt from your mind for fear of blocking a miracle. When the miracle doesn't come, and you are crushed, they want you to turn to the person who withheld the miracle but refuses to tell you why (e.g., where you erred in the asking, the cleansing of self, asking the wrong person to join you in praying, not knowing if this person's life is less worth living and thus worth sacrificing in His eyes) for comfort.

Ain't that some bullshit.

Sorry to say this, but the moment my father called to let me know my mom was no longer living, I immediately ceased my belief in God. Don't judge, it wasn't on purpose, it just left my body, and I've only continued to find reasons why He doesn't exist. If He is all-powerful and could have done something to save my mom's life and didn't, then He is incredibly cruel. If He chose not to for some greater purpose, then why was her life less valuable than that purpose, and why does that purpose have to be unknown? If I'm supposed to learn a lesson from this, then why make it impossible to access? If God is in control of everything, then He is making a choice for me to experience this, yet I don't know why He chose to let her die, at this time, in this way. There are studies that show that if a parent punishes a child for a reason that is unknown to the child, it is an ineffective punishment at the least and torture at the worst.

People also like to credit God for performing miracles, for the presence of the good things that happen in our lives. To me, this means that if He is responsible for the good, then He is responsible for the bad. So, I could choose to believe in a God who is all-knowing, all-powerful yet cruel and illusive, or I can accept what feels more correct to me—and honestly is more kind to those who do believe in God, in my opinion—and acknowledge that there is no God.

My therapist wants me to have hope. I told her I have none, and I don't believe it serves us well. Hope hinders us from preparing for alternate possibilities. She asked me to explore hope vs. expectations. Hence the above. So what do I hope for? Hmm. It would have to be minuscule enough to not need expectation coupled with it—like, I hope you're happy, but if you're not, I'll be alright. But that's nothing to live for. So what hope do I have for the future? I anticipate nothing specific. I expect that one day I will be able to live without so much pain and feeling the black hole my mother's death caused, but I don't hope for that. Hope implies happiness and joy, and I don't feel happy or joyous for the future. So what do I fuckin' hope for?! I am racking my brain. I hope my children (if I have any) believe my Mom was real and that the stories of her are true. I hope they don't think she's an urban legend. I hope they can love her, but I understand if that's not possible since they'll have no real experience with her. It would still hurt, but I can understand that. Any other hopes? I hope to make a lot of money. My actions are not currently aligned with that, but since hope can be all willey nilley, why not hope for it? Debt is dumb. Debt causes stress which lowers IQ and I need all my brain capacity to stay alive. So, I hope money does not become an object in the future. I've got some hopes. Happy now? Is my current state of life better now?

I get it. Being left with no hope is devastating. Hope is what is keeping a lot of folks alive: the hope for a better tomorrow, the hope for a better job, the hope for a happy family. Living without hope makes life feel kinda pointless and scary. Life is not nearly as clean and organized without hope. I'm not advocating for a life without hope; I don't want you to live without hope. I'm just speaking my truth. What you choose to do with it is really not my concern.

Do you see now why 'The Matrix' is so mind-blowing?! It is very thought-provoking. Think about the movie. Their actual physical world is fucked. There are still fields of humans being mined. But what are Neo and the others really working towards? Those who have taken the red pill will eventually overthrow the computers by……. doing something that wipes them out while maintaining whatever part of them sustains the current fields of humans so they don't die. And then? Awaken the…babies first? Maybe awaken some adults they think will handle it well, so there's someone to take care of the babies? That's not their policy, so we'll see how that goes. The ones who want to remain in the ugly physical reality are good to go. The ones who want to remain ignorant…they can't go back to that make-believe world because the computers have to be gone, or else they'll take back over. So, you gotta…kill them? Build them a Disneyland to live in until they die? Would that even work, given that there's no sun? How do people live happily in a ravished land where they don't want to be?

As challenging and complicated as that is, I do think it's better than being liquified and fed to each other. Or maybe it isn't for you, if you didn't know about it.

I promise I'm not trying to be a Debbie Downer. I'm just saying that once you know reality, you are forced to face it. And that brings a shitload of other challenges with it. It's not pretty. It's not fun. It's just real.

I can see why belief in God would be helpful in these moments. I don't want to take your hope away! I'd much rather live with hope. I just don't have hope in that construct.

It's funny because I have been known to be the friend or colleague who finds the silver lining and makes things work in the face of obstacles. My persistence is something I'm proud of and something that's gotten me far in life. I wish I could see the faces and hear the thoughts of my friends, family and former coworkers as they read this. Yeah, this is also me.

At the time, removing God and belief in God from my life felt so natural. As I described, I didn't really have a choice in the matter. I now realize that this was Major Loss #2. Faith, faith in God, and belonging to a faith community were such central parts of my life and my identity that losing all of those in addition to losing the most essential person to my being, further contributed to my experience of loss. As you process loss or commit to being there for someone through loss, it is helpful to be aware of complicating factors. Even if you don't know exactly what they are, know that complicating factors exist and that they play a role in the response.

CHAPTER 2

What Doesn't Kill You Makes You Stronger

If you think or have ever said, "This will make you stronger," well, have I got a chapter for you.

It is true that if I were forced to use only my left hand for a month or even the rest of my life, my left hand and arm would get stronger. My capabilities on that side would greatly increase, probably even beyond what I can imagine possible.

It is also true that if I broke my left leg and had it cast and had to use crutches for 3 months, my right leg would get stronger. My already shapely and muscular calves would bulge and be able to scale mountains. In fact, my arms would get stronger, too, from all the crutching. Especially if I kept up my current regimen of daily 2-mile walks.

But what about my right arm after a month or lifetime of un-use? Or my left leg after 3 months in a cast?

Not vivid enough for you?

There are some people who say that pain, suffering and hardship make us stronger. But they won't come right out and say, "Suffering makes you stronger," because that sounds mean. They'll do it like, "You'll come out the other end of this stronger," or "You are so strong; you'll get through this."

To them, I say, "I hope your mom dies slowly and painfully over 10 years so that you can get stronger." What? Did I sound too mean? Sorry, not sorry. Don't be mad at me or look at me all different now! I told you I was going to be honest! I'm not being mean! Getting stronger is a good thing. Okay… let's see. If that one didn't land for you… Maybe your mom is older, and you are beginning to accept that she won't always be here. Or you don't have a relationship with your mom. Then to you I say, "I hope you struggle to have a child, that it takes years and years, and then finally your dream comes true, and your sweet baby is born. They are so sweet and cuddly and smile up at you with all the joy in their eyes that they can muster, and it truly warms your heart and makes life the happiest it's ever been. Then, you look up and realize that your child is crying all the time, and you find out they are in pain and suffering every minute of their day. I hope you watch them grow for 10 years, and in each of those years, their pain increases, and you don't know what to do to help them. Finally, your child dies slowly and painfully. But! You now are so much stronger. Think of how much more you can do with your newfound strength." If you don't like that, then don't try to tell me that my mom's death is good for me, helpful for me or will make me stronger.

Is that extra strength even worth it? At what cost does it come? If I had my choice, I'd rather stay right-hand dominant with regular strength in my left hand. No problem with that at all.

CHAPTER 3

STRUGGLING

Sometimes I wake up feeling crappy. And I wonder, is this how my day is going to be? Is my mood this morning related to why I woke up soaked in sweat? Or is it related to my meds, dreams, biology, nightmares or some combination of 2 or more? Is it in my hands to determine how my day will turn out? Typically, I believe we cannot choose our feelings, but we can and should choose our actions. So just because we feel crappy does not mean that we should act *'crappily'* toward others. Now, having struggled and battled and survived depression in the past, I also now have the recognition that one can feel a certain way and not have as much control over their actions as I once thought they did. There are times when the chemical imbalance of depression clouds the ability to choose movement over inaction, e.g., getting out of bed. I have also experienced how anxiety clouds rational thought, so although action is possible, it may not be based in or proportionate to reality. And now that grief is involved...lord have mercy.

So do I have a choice on whether or not my day continues in this vein? Honestly, sometimes, yes and sometimes no.

So What *Do* I Do?

Everyone is different. Period. I believe grief is incurable, but if you really love someone and you want to make it about them, you can be there for them as much as you can. I'm going to give some tips because it would have been helpful to not have to educate people while I was going through it and because I know that most of us actually want to help. I'm going to go against my nature and speak in absolutes. Not everyone will experience things how I did, but the larger point will be helpful no matter what.

A. Time means everything, and time means nothing. Be in it for the long haul.

At the beginning (I'd say the first week), I got lots of texts and calls. I was somehow able to respond to all of them, I think. Then I got numb. For you, time continues. For those in grief, often time does not. That loss is something those in grief are now forced to live with for <u>the rest of their lives</u>. It took me 7 months to say the word "dead" and to this day (1.5 years at the time I'm typing this), I still don't truly believe she is gone. Throw away your notions of timelines.

B. Keep checking in, and remember that it's not about you, so you *must* give some grace.

This is now something that they will live with **for the rest of their lives**. Let that sink in. Most people only check in once after it happens and then are ready to move past the discomfort. Keep checking in. We need you.

CHAPTER 4

A HELPFUL LIST

The list below does not take into account any specific cultural or religious customs.

I am going to assume that you care enough about the person to want to show them that you care. So preface each of these with, "If you care about the person and…". Please read through each list so you can see what has purposefully *not* been given to you and for additional tips on what not to do.

1) You are not very close (emotionally) to the one who is grieving.

    A. Check to see if the family has made any requests for how to show your support. If they have asked for flowers, donations, etc., to be sent somewhere, <u>do that</u>. Do not make up your own thing. There is no need to be creative or fancy. That just adds stress. They already told you what they want. Do it!

    B. Do not send flowers to their home unless the family requested it. Flowers clutter, flowers die and must be cared for and disposed of, and there are others who are closer to the family that will give flowers.

C. Do not send flowers to their job. Many people are able to use work as a distraction, and your flowers force a painful reality in a place where they may have a useful diversion or where they may have chosen to keep the loss private.

D. Send a card. Note that the family may or may not read the card, but that doesn't matter. Find a simple card that only speaks to your sorrow at the loss and does not include words of consolation. Oftentimes, what we think is comforting, is insulting to someone who is grieving. Even if the family is religious, some within the family may not be (and haven't told you), and some may be struggling with the higher power's role in all of it, so you run the risk of isolating them further. Better to be safe than sorry. Remember, it's not about you. You are doing this so *they* feel better, not you.

E. If you still want to do more, enclose money. Money may not be needed, but it can always be used.

F. Do not drop by their home. Nobody asked for your presence, so don't burden them with having to entertain you.

G. Do not expect, require or even desire a response to anything you do. It is overwhelming to have someone you love die. It is downright cruel to say you are there to

24

support and then want the person who is drowning to pat you on the back for reaching out to them.

2) You are kind of emotionally close and in physical proximity.

   A. If you have to ask them if you can visit their home, follow the guidelines above.

3) You are close to them emotionally and in physical proximity.

   A. Visit as soon as possible. Let them know you are coming and ask if that day and time are okay.

   B. If you see no flowers or plants have been sent to their home, bring some on your next visit.

   C. Sit with them and say nothing.

   D. Sit with them and talk about how much this sucks.

   E. Ask them if there's anything they want to talk about. Be prepared that they may not know what they want, but it's okay for you to ask.

   F. Do not ask, "How are you doing?" You know how they're doing. Shitty! Say, "I love you, I'm here for you." Let them take it from there.

   G. Play unobtrusive music or turn on the TV to something lightweight so there's background noise that is not annoying. You know what they like/don't like.

H. Bring snacks and foods that do not require anything more than a microwave.

I. If you see things that need to be done around the home (e.g., washing dishes, throwing away dead flowers), do that, and don't ask for permission.

J. If they are talking about having a service, offer specific help based on your skill sets (e.g., typing up the program, reaching out to whom they want to have a role in the service). If you don't have the skills, talk with another of your shared friends and see who can help with those tasks.

K. If unwanted visitors show up, entertain them. You're in a better position to make polite chit-chat. Also, make a sign or let people know when they arrive that visits are limited to 10 minutes.

4) You are close to them emotionally but not in physical proximity.

A. Call as soon as possible. Let them know you love them and are so sorry they are going through this and that it sucks. Do not try to find comforting words or offer words of consolation. As stated earlier, often, those are the words that hurt most. Keep it short unless they continue the conversation.

B. If you have shared friends who are in physical proximity, reach out to them to see what else you can do (e.g., send flowers to their home, help with a service, send a meal to their home).

C. Do not text or ask, "How are you doing?" You know how they're doing. Shitty! Say, "I love you" or "Thinking of you." Let them take it from there.

D. As listed above, do not send flowers to their job.

All of these strategies will need to be used. You will have to use context clues, emotional awareness, and read body language and listen to what they are telling you they need in that actual moment to know what to do. I'm not saying this is easy at all—I'm just telling you what I have found to be true and helpful.

As a reminder, they will be dealing with this for the rest of their lives. Checking in does not end after the first week or after the service or after the first year. Your role in supporting them must be nuanced and be determined by your relationship with them.

CHAPTER 5

HUMAN CONNECTION

I heard on a podcast (The Myth of Closure, *On Being with Krista Trippet* with Pauline Boss, December 2018) that "sadness is treated with human connection." Loss causes the ultimate sadness. We need you to connect with us or we lose touch with reality and with the goodness of life that still exists. You are **necessary** for our healing.

Now here's a biggie. As you check in and keep checking in, you absolutely have got to remember that it is not about you. Remember, the person you care about has experienced something that has shattered their world, changed their understanding of some things, and they are reeling. Remember, your timeline is irrelevant, so even if they seem fine week 1 or 2, month 3 could be hell, or maybe only certain memories or special days send them reeling. For one of my family members, it wasn't until year 2 that she stopped being comforted by her belief that this was all God's plan, and she started really hurting and missing my mom, even though she still believed it to be true that God knew what was best. Because you don't know what's going on inside of them, you never know which version of them will be receiving the love you are trying to show. If they are in a rough moment, experiencing anxiety, feeling overwhelmed or hopeless, they may be rude, mean, short, cryptic, may yell, curse, cry, may start laughing, they may hang up on you, or they may say nothing or not reply to you at all. They may tell you something they don't like about you that you find to be completely unrelated to the conversation at hand. In those moments, call on the strength of your ancestors, take a yoga breath, count to 10 or do whatever works for you. Breathe in, "This is not about me…", breathe out, "show ___ *(insert loved one's name)* some grace." Do it several times if needed. Consider that their reaction is an incredibly heart-breaking response to trauma. Then listen again or re-read that text. Sometimes the frustration or anger has built up and though the packaging is faulty, there is a message in there, and if they are trying to tell you something, you don't want to miss it, and they need you to hear it.

Other ways I could have been helped in the midst of my darkest days:

1) Never ask, "How are you?" I'm always horrible. My mom is dead. Even if I'm fake smiling, I feel like shit. A better question is, "Is there anything you want to talk about?"

2) Don't force me to talk about her. It hurts too much to talk about her when I don't want to. It does not help me to remember the good; that makes me feel worse. Your good memories are exactly why I miss her so much right now and why I want to keep ignoring reality.

3) Find another way to show me you love me. I did not know what I needed, and that's all I knew. That was hella frustrating for me too! If you love me, you'll pick up a book, phone a friend, get some tips from somebody who ain't me.

4) Sometimes, I just need to vent. You can't solve this. It is so hard to just sit in pain with someone and do nothing to make it better. With loss, you are contending with the fact that if you cannot bring the person back to life, you cannot solve the problem. But! You can do things to help the person in it. Venting is huge. It took me almost a year to be able to express my feelings, and just the act of putting them into words and saying them aloud to another person was therapeutic. Where it went bad was when the other person said something back to me that made me feel worse (yes, I know she wouldn't want to see me so sad and so angry and so stuck, yet I am. And now I feel horrible that on top of all that, I'm also not living up to her memory. Thanks.).

During a series of my bad days, my best friend reached out and actually supported me using some of the strategies that had helped me previously, and I lashed out at her via text (yes, she has the receipts, and she's still choosing to be my BFF). I wrote several text scrolls of reply and told her she had made me feel worse. It wasn't kind, but I was having a moment where I was tired of editing myself and just wanted to say what I wanted to say. After I pushed send, I simultaneously felt relief that the feelings I'd been holding in were off my chest and I immediately felt physically burdensome regret at how I'd spoken to my best friend—someone who also loved my mom, someone who has literally been there for me since day 1 (our moms were best friends), and someone who has only ever been above and beyond kind and thoughtful to me (she's an amazingly good person, not exaggerating)—and I was scared at what she'd say back, how long I'd have to wait for a reply and the anxiety of waiting, and wondering if I'd ruined our relationship. She wrote me back not even a minute later and said, "I apologize for making you feel like… [a lot of good stuff] …I want to respect your feelings and needs." I do not know how she had the wisdom and showed me so much grace at that moment, but I cannot thank her enough for not reacting to me as I'd reacted to her. That immediate apology and her bottom line statement allowed me to open up about all the situations and feelings that I had bottled up. Those feelings had nothing to do with her and she was not the reason why I was triggered and reacted as I did, and throughout all of the follow-up conversation, she was empathetic, jumped to my defense, thanked *me* for expressing my feelings, never asked for an apology at the way I'd spoken to her, and ended the entire thing with "I love you."

Thank you, BFF. You are the perfect example of how to truly be there for a loved one who is grieving. I sincerely apologize for taking it all out on you. Thank you for being my safe space and for continuing to be my BFF.

So, they need you forever, they may treat you like shit for a moment, there may be a message in that—so don't miss that—and if not, that's ok too, but please, still come back.

Now, here is a word to make sure people are safe in their relationships. When I talk about people lashing out and you being willing to take it, I mean that this is something they did not do before the loss. You know them and are now seeing different reactions than what you have always known. If they were snapping at you like that when they were not grieving and in the midst of heartbreak, then why are you friends? That's unacceptable. Second, it is never okay for their pain and lashing out to include physical violence towards you or anyone else. Period. That requires help beyond the scope of this book, so please contact The National Domestic Violence Hotline, available 24/7 at 800-799-SAFE (7233), to get help in those situations.

CHAPTER 6

IF YOU ARE GRIEVING

Things I Learned to Help in Your Grief:

1) It fucking sucks. I'm sorry you're experiencing this. Know that you are not alone and even if your experience differs from mine, both of our experiences are valid and normal.

2) If you're reading this, you're amazing. To be at a place where you can read and comprehend...take a moment and acknowledge how much that took to get here. Every baby step that led you to this page...I see you.

3) Read the tips I give to people who want to help us. This may help normalize how you're feeling and what you're experiencing, and if you need to, you can make a copy of a page and send it discreetly or boldly to someone.

4) Get help from someone who is <u>certified</u> in grief, not someone who lists grief as one of their specialty areas on a website— certified vs. specializes. People may have studied grief in school, but what they were taught is a snippet of what the real experience is. A grief group may also be beneficial. You get a better understanding of common reactions to grief, you learn

specific solutions and ideas for how to keep living, and you can find a community of people who may relate to you. For me, I left my grief group because I could not handle hearing about others' problems at that time, and the group that worked out for me to attend was faith-based (even though I inquired before starting if it was, and they said it wasn't), but I know others who felt much more comfortable in the group setting and got a lot of assistance that way.

I had a couple therapists share some things from the Jewish culture, and a Jewish friend of mine whose father died a few months before my mom confirmed them. They shared a few practices with me and these practices are incredibly sensitive to grieving and respectful of the reality of the process. There are two things in particular that if I'd known in advance maybe would have helped me feel better about my own reaction.

I am not a member of the Jewish community, and my explanation of these is based on how I understood what they shared with me and what I found to be extremely helpful.

1) Sitting Shiva

When my mom first passed, I felt so much pressure to reply to everyone and make them feel better about the loss. She was known widely and had made a huge impact in our faith community and throughout her professional life. So there were many who were mourning. Our nuclear family was my dad, my younger sister and me, and it felt like most people wanted to make contact with at least 1 of us soon after. We chose not to have a funeral because we had held a celebration while she was alive that she had planned and that was 3 months prior, so it felt redundant to have a funeral. Plus, I don't think any of us were emotionally capable of executing what is required to make a funeral happen. I think that compounded the number of people who kept reaching out, wanting to talk and at varying times. I am an introvert and not a phone person, but at first, the barrage of texts was ok, and I had a stock reply that kept things at arms' distance. But as things continued throughout that month and my first level of shock wore off, I got crazy overwhelmed by the daily messages that piled up; the cards sent that I never replied to, the hundreds of thank you cards I'd been raised to send that went unsent, and I began to feel like I was failing my mom's legacy of polite, thoughtful children.

The therapists helped assuage my guilt by giving me some context of sitting shiva. In Jewish culture, it is understood that the one who is mourning the most intimately is under a crushing enough burden that having to also respond individually to all the caring friends and family is just too much. So everyone comes to them. And brings food. And talks to each other, so you don't have to carry on every conversation. It's also for a set amount of time, so it doesn't keep extending on and on removing your ability to have time to sit with your own damn feelings. I'm not fully sure how to transpose that to non-Jewish mourners, but for me, at least knowing that people were aware enough to create a system like that let me cut myself some slack, and I stopped feeling pressure to reply to everything, and I stopped trying to make others feel better. They could either (try to) comfort me or keep it moving.

2) The Practice of Headstones

In my first session with my grief-certified therapist (and then surprisingly in a conversation later that week with my friend), I told her how much more distraught previous therapy attempts had made me because I needed a safe place to discuss my feelings and they were ready for me to move on. For example, 9 months after my mother's passing, I still was not ready/able to admit or believe she was gone. My previous therapist and a psychiatrist made me feel bad for that, and they both said I was dishonoring her memory because of that. Way to make somebody jump-start healing, right?! She was thankfully appalled and let me know that in Jewish culture, they don't put the headstone on the grave until a year later, in recognition that it takes time to come to grips with the fact that your loved one is gone and is not coming back.

What so many people don't understand is that although many of us want a different reality, there is a way to acknowledge our pain and our present reality without making us feel like shit. She didn't bring my mom back to life, but she also didn't make me feel worse, and she helped slow my heart rate in my moment of despair. Yes, this fucking sucks. Yes, people have said fucked up things. Also yes, others have gone through loss, and they have felt similarly enough to know that what you are feeling is normal and what you need is time and our support in <u>this</u> way and not <u>that</u>. And I took a breath and believed her.

PART C

JOURNAL ENTRIES

I used a notebook to first write this book by hand. My initial desire for the book was to give people insight into what it's like to grieve and to give tips on how to help someone who is grieving. Sometime during that writing process, I also began to use the notebook as a journal. I've decided to include some of the journal entries as further insight into my experience and because in re-reading those entries, I'm surprised by the lucidity of what I wrote for others' benefit.

Warning: there are points in here that are pretty dark. Do with that warning what you will. Know that I am under the care of a licensed professional and I am okay.

Date Unknown

Sometimes the icky feelings won't stop. I've felt off for days and I don't know how long this is going to last. I'm super sad, I have no energy, I don't want to do anything, yet I'm tired of doing nothing. I'm restless and rest-less.

I applied for a job yesterday to see if that would help. And when I say "yesterday," I mean it took me a month to work up the courage to apply for a job I'm sure will be too stressful for me; it took me a couple of weeks looking at the job description and company values to wrap my mind around how I can fit in; it took a couple days to complete the online application, and then I discovered a resume was requested; it then took me a couple days to rework my resume to fit a career change and entry-level position; and yesterday, that process was complete, so I pushed submit. Last night I was freaking out, scared they would contact me - particularly irrational given it was a Friday night - and equally frightened I wouldn't get a response at all. My anxiety is at a peak, and I'm not sure how to get it down. I'm taking my meds (prescribed by a doctor who doesn't get grief or believe me when I tell her my symptoms, so who knows if that matters, but I am doing it), I'm taking daily walks and exercising (a known stress reliever, and I'm sore as proof), I'm sharing some emotions with my husband and sister and getting some relief from that pressure valve, I'm forcing myself to go out of the house and to fun events, I'm replying when friends or family reach out, dammit I'm fighting my ass off yet I still sit here completely deflated and unable to enjoy the gorgeous sun streaming through my window directly onto my skin. WTF. Just WTF.

It doesn't take much to fuck up the delicate ecosystem of gently balanced emotions and activities. One minute I'm bouncing along, making rapid progress and feeling like I'll be a member of society again. Then I get a text from _____, and I'm set down a path of negative, painful, recurring thoughts that I can't seem to parachute away from. I remember everyone I thought was a friend whom I thought I could count on, and I'm hurt again that they've abandoned me when I needed them most. I write and rehearse speeches or texts or letters I want to give them and then scrap them because why put energy into people that don't care enough to even try. So I spend a ton of energy pushing away thoughts and feelings I think are unhelpful to my day at hand, and it ends up leaving me totally spent. I'm starting to agree with my therapist that I have to feel these horrible things rather than push them away to emerge at a later date in a much more harmful way (picture me walking through my office a year from now and randomly falling to my knees, letting out a scream that echoes off the walls, falling to my side curling into a ball rocking back and forth muttering, "Why did Becky throw out the coffee already?"), but then I'm struggling with how to feel these things right now. I've pushed away my emotions for so long. And I'm trying to set boundaries in my relationships. I don't want to have a "Come to Jesus" conversation with everyone I'm upset with. So I want to get over that. What's the right way to feel the feels, think the thoughts, and then let go of what to let go of?

And right on cue, my husband texts me, "It's show a lot of love to KC day!!!!!" with a super cute bear blowing kisses. Alllllllmost makes you think there is a God whispering in his ear that I'm in the middle of journaling about being in the middle of some shit! But then you remember, if He's responsible for the good, then He's also responsible for the bad. So you put a pin in those thoughts, re-read the happy, love-filled, insightful text, and decide to stop writing, shower, and strap on your parachute.

4/14/19

Yesterday I was able to say "Mom." My husband asked me a few times where I'd gotten a small backpack I took on our anniversary trip. We'd been looking for the right one for at least a year. Small but big enough to fit some things. Fancy enough to be worn by an adult but casual enough to wear with jeans. After several times of ignoring/diverting a response, I finally said, "It was my Mom's." And I didn't break down, so I added more, "I found it when we were packing up her things. It's perfect!" Somehow, I didn't collapse into depression or feel crushing sadness. I had a small smile at how she had the unique talent of finding great items and how I was happy to have this bag to carry and remember her and think about where she may have worn it to. I was really careful with it, however. Didn't want to get any stains on the leather or mess it up in any way. The thought of a paint stain or bird poop on it caused my heart to pound while I was walking around using it. It's perfect for what I need and want but I don't want to use it for fear of messing it up. I want to preserve and utilize/honor it at the same time. It did make me happy to have a moment of pleasant recollection. It makes me want to think of her more and let her smile be my smile. It would be amazing if I could do that.

The Warriors are in the playoffs again. I'm watching their game wearing the shirt my mom got at the 2015 finals run. The Warriors went on a crazy, fun run in the 2nd quarter and pulled ahead by 23 with some awesome 3s, dunks and great teamwork on display. These are moments when I loved calling her and talking about our team, good things we are seeing, where there's room for improvement, when she's going to another game. So usually, I push all thoughts of her out of my head so I can enjoy the game without sobbing. And I get a headache from the effort but eventually forget that I'd wanted to call her. So now, I wait. I'm caught in this place of having a pleasant memory for the 2nd time ever, but wondering if I'm going to plunge and not be able to get up tomorrow. I feel ok right now, though and that surprises me greatly. I'm worried about if I'll be able to sleep and what kind of nightmares I may have, but maybe this is the start of something new? Or if not, at least it's a different kind of day, and I should appreciate this moment? It's sad to be scared of happiness, yet that's my reality.

OMG Mother, Warriors were up by 31 points. Clippers somehow came back and beat them by 4. What?!

Date Unknown

If I have idle time, my mind begins to drift. It's pretty much always a dangerous thing because it only takes 2 seconds or a sequence of 2 connected thoughts to have my mind drift to her or to a future that will occur without her. Sometimes, I think about how much I don't care about anything else besides that void, and I get angry that people make me talk about or think about anything else. Nothing else matters, I want to scream at people. But I love them, and I know I should care, and maybe a part of me can still care, so I push forward with pretending.

I watched an interview with Cal Newport, who talked about digital minimalism. Humanity has changed to a point where we look at our phones to fill idle time and keep us from being bored. He talked about how dangerous that is for the brain to not have downtime and how we need time with our own thoughts. There have been plenty of people talking about our new addiction to phones, how we touch them hundreds of times a day and are driven by the designers of apps that make us think we must stay connected at all times. I believe them. I believe it is harmful. However, I am more scared of being alone with my own thoughts, so I keep myself distracted at all times - phone, games, TV, movies, podcasts - whatever it takes. I'd much rather fill my mind with others' thoughts than my own. I was one to limit my phone usage to a few times a day, barely at all during work hours. And I'd removed TV from my home in recognition of how much time it consumes and how it dissuades you from your hobbies, creativity, thinking. Fuck all that now, though! Distract me all you want, big brother.

I hope to be distracted by a job soon. Don't get me wrong, I'm terrified of responsibility, I don't think I can wake up multiple days in a row at an appointed time, I don't like people right now, and I'm depressed and anxious at all times. However, I think it would be helpful to have a reason to leave the house. I'm scared as all get out, though. What a dichotomy. Better yet, what is a good word for when the brain is fractured or splintered like a windshield nicked by a rock? More than 2. What a trifecta. What a quarter. What a symphony of confusion.

Interlude

So, I recognized that I needed therapy (even I can laugh at that sentence!). Finding a therapist was one of the hardest things I've had to do. The insurance I had was very limited; they required pre-authorization to get therapy or a psychiatrist, but I didn't have a primary care physician since I'd just moved from another state, plus I was super depressed, so doing all the work to navigate and research took days to build up the energy to do anything and then I was drained to the max from talking to people or researching and hitting dead ends. It's clear that America does not value people over profit.

Return to the entry

If I were to quit a job without notice, I'd be labeled "unprofessional". Unprofessional really means you care about self over company, and we've been trained that that is negative. Generous companies give 5 days off for grief. That is the standard allowance. Some companies give none. Hourly, minimum-wage jobs only pay you for what you work. As you can see, that doesn't cover anything in the grand scheme of things. The time allocated is not sufficient enough to plan a service, complete all the paperwork that accompanies death, notify and speak with all your friends and family and theirs (I don't believe in using social media to notify), travel to where your loved one or family could be - and we haven't even started processing what actually happened.

A society that views its citizens as a commodity would provide actual resources to guide people through such a jarring time. There would be a month of days that could be used flexibly over the following 365 days, and any time the person needed to come in late or leave early because of processing or crushing sadness, they could. And rather than be worried about if someone were abusing that, we'd be more concerned that people who needed it wouldn't use it. Offices would create oases within the building where people could go when they needed a moment to gather themselves. Where there would be no embarrassment for not working for 30 minutes to write or meditate or call a friend to help share the load.

These are great practices for grief and imagine how much they would help our work environments overall! We need a culture that considers the sanity and well-being of its people as a priority. Professional means person-centered; it is understood that there is no company without the people, and there is no quality work without well people. We need to stop pushing people to suppress their real emotions because we know that only makes them worse.

May 11, 2019

I am back at the beach (hear an audible ahhhhh exhale). I've chosen what I think is a more secluded spot. Plus, it's pretty early for a beach day. The forecast said it would be cloudy, but the temp is still 83, and I haven't been here in weeks, so I decided to come anyway. Great decision. The clouds have burned away. My umbrella is perfectly positioned (after ooone little tumble), the breeze is divine, and the sound of the ocean is forcing my breathing to sync with its rhythm. In other words, I am happy.

Happy is a weird word to use. Maybe "content" is more accurate. Yeah! Content.

Mother's Day is tomorrow. That doggone holiday is damn hard to avoid. Every commercial for an otherwise normal product is now the perfect gift for the favorite woman in your life (which I guess is me? Yeah, right, it's always gonna be my sister, lol). I keep literally shaking the day out of my head and doing some serious dissociation when I hear the words M.D. It's been working, I think. That plus starting a new med that seems to be controlling my anxiety better. Which is a Godsend (metaphorically speaking) because being denied disability means I was at my wit's end for how to be. How to exist, live and be. And continuing the good news, I got a job! It's been incredible, actually. I was <u>terrified</u> throughout the process, but my girls literally willed me and coached me through it. They talked me through each step, literally shimmied positivity into my spirit, and conducted mock interviews with me. And this is for a PT, no experience needed position, at minimum wage. So yeah, the money sucks, and I need more income, which is stressful AF, but! I can wake up at a certain time each day, get somewhere on time, learn some routine skills, and smile at strangers! I'm amazed. And mother f'in exhausted. I work my few hours, come home, and pass the fuck out for the rest of the day. I'm useless at everything else. I haven't been able to write, go grocery shopping, listen to my podcasts, talk with family or friends, and I have had to cancel 2 doctor's appointments...child, nothing. I need so much sleep. But yes, it is making me happy to be useful, bring in money to our household, and fake it with people who may never know my history and have fun with this great group of people. Also, if you can afford to, tip. Baristas work hard for it, and we need it.

My sis and I decided to make a meal in our respective homes tomorrow from our mom's recipes. It's too costly to travel and be together tomorrow, so we're going to FaceTime and cook together. The idea came to me last month when my husband asked how I wanted to spend M Day. I'm glad he brought it up early because that gave me time to think before being bombarded with the ads. I told my sis the idea, and she loved it. So, we're making mac n cheese, baked beans, broccoli and cheesecake. Plenty for 2 people in each household. I also secretly made my mom's peach cobbler on Wednesday, froze it, and shipped it to my sis. It should arrive tonight. It's my sis's second fav dessert that my mom made, and I like making (and eating) it, so I figured that would be a nice treat. It's funny because she's been telling me all week that big sisters are the best, and she doesn't even know about this treat yet. That's bringing me a lot of joy, hehehe!

Last week in therapy, I told Queen Z that I usually send about 10-15 cards for this holiday. We have so many aunts, cousins, moms of god kids, grandmothers, etc., who are special to us, and I like honoring them. But I told her I got permission to take this year off. The thought of combing through sentimental BS and words of love for Moms makes me gag. Then she suggested, "Why don't you have your husband get the cards you want to send this year? He's a problem solver. He wants to help. All you'll have to do is cover the words and sign your name." BRILLIANT! I lit up like the sun I'm sitting under. Because I do appreciate those who have been here throughout this year in particular, and I want them to know that. And now they will! I told hubs, and he was so down. Thank you, Love! Told my sis, too so she could have her husband do the same. She was so happy too! Brilliant, brilliant. I'm giving away secrets I paid good money for, but if you're in a similar predicament, this solution is a life saver! Thank you, Queen Z.

Date Unknown

I've been having nightmares the last couple nights. In my dream last night, I was at our childhood home gathering a few things of my mom's, which made me have to stay there a few moments longer than my sis. I'd already gone through most of her things, so it was taking longer to make sure I hadn't left any gems behind. My father was following me and trying to make small talk, which was lighting a small fire underneath me and causing my blood to simmer slowly and then boil. I didn't want to make small talk. If we were going to talk, I wanted to talk about her. Or maybe not talk about her because that hurt too much too. I kept going off on him, just exploding, but then things would stop, and it seemed like I'd only gone off on him in my mind. I kept juggling that I had nothing to say, and if he didn't get that, that it would be a waste of energy, and me going off would just endanger my ability to get what I needed. At the same time, he kept trying to give me a wad of cash, which I didn't want to take but I knew it would help me. So I was wrestling with that in my mind too. I ended up with a couple of shirts and handheld things, so I looked for a small bag to put them in. Found a mini backpack, which I was thinking about how I didn't need it, but decided to fit everything in there anyway so I could leave. I struggled to get things to fit, while he kept making small talk. I can't really remember what he was saying, but it was more of a steady stream of chit chat. "How are things? Things are going well for me. Been doing x, y, z. Thinking about t, u, v. Can you hear the drone of my voice?" Um, hm, yeah... [Ahhhh! I'm boiling again.] So, I finally got everything and stepped out the door, and the metal staircase disconnected from the ground, so one end was connected to the ledge outside the front door, and the other was whipping in the air. I'm hanging off the end and trying to pull my legs up and get my feet on the bottom rung. The stairs have now flattened, so each stair is now just a rung on an ambulating ladder. My dad grabs the end of the railing that is connected to the house, and I think he's trying to steady it so I'm not twisting and turning and almost getting flung off to my death hundreds of feet below. But he keeps holding the rail like reins and whipping it, so it causes more shock waves of movement, and my arms are straining with the effort of holding on. He's shouting things I can't hear because of my fight response and adrenaline, but his face looks concerned, and it seems like he's trying to give me tips and wants me to make it. But he's whipping the railing and making it worse and harder for me to hold on. I finally am able to pull my legs up and get a foot on the bottom rung, and I leapfrog my arms to a higher section of the rung and physically pull myself inch by inch. [My shoulders are aching now as I write this, so I must have been working out in my sleep for real.] I look to my left and see a tightrope leading to the way down, where a tour bus with my sis and others is impatiently waiting for me to finish so we can get out of there. I can see the tops of the trees and decide to just walk the tightrope to a pole and get down. Next thing I know, we're on the tour bus, and we're driving off.

I woke up so distressed and sad and needing to cry or something. I started contemplating what all that means and what it was about and what I should do with all that. Dang. There's my alarm for work. Snoozing that. I gotta get this negativity out so I can pretend to have a good day. I laid there feeling like drippy shit for a while and really didn't want to take this negativity with me or have to tell someone about it in order to get it off of my chest and into the world so it could float away. I have therapy in 2 days, so I'll talk with her about it. But I needed to get it out now! And then I remembered, that's what this notebook is for. So here you go. Welcome to my grief-driven dreams. Ok. Time to get ready for work. Mother fucker!

May 2019

My sis asked me to do some future planning with her, and as part of our activities, we discussed what makes us happy. Rather, she did. When it got to my turn, I passed. I can't think of the future. Or happiness. I've reached a stage where I'm okay with the present. And I do everything I can to stay in that moment - not remembering the past or contemplating the future. That gets painful real quick, plus I can't imagine it. The future is a haze through which I can't navigate, a path unseen. Then we get to happiness. What the fuck is that? So now that our conversation is over and my mind is at peace (we're spending a couple days at a spa on a beach), so it's wandering to "what is happiness" and what is happiness' role is in my life. I'm not sure. I have times when I'm happy, I think. I smile. I laugh. I feel content in a moment. But am I happy? I don't think so. I think I'm a zombie with a happy facade on. But I don't mean to diminish the times when I may have felt happy. Maybe I really was. I'm just not, in this moment. So maybe I can't imagine happiness. I can only experience it in the moment. Or nah. My optimism wants me to have been happy. My realism is pulling me back to center. WTH! Who knew tranquility and hope could put me in such a negative mind space? I feel icky, and I want to retreat again. Have 5 days under my covers with the sound of the ocean piped into my ears, and my phone turned off and downstairs in a drawer somewhere. It's one of those kinda days...

Date Unknown

People keep telling me that they love me. Rather, people keep telling me that I should accept their pitiful expressions of selfishness because they love me. What the hell are we teaching people that love is?

I am so fed up with people telling me that their self-centered behavior is love. Or that their hurtful actions don't actually matter because, in addition, they love me. Seriously, what the hell, people? Three people close to me and with different types of relationships with me are currently doing that circle dance with me, and I'm way over it. As I look back at the history of our relationships, I realize they have always been selfish. Their actions always showed that they thought foremost of their own feelings and desires. In the past, I prided myself on how accepting I was and how strong my friends and family were. I liked the people with strong personalities who sometimes offended people because of their strong convictions. I like when people know who they are and what they want and are unapologetic about that. I also felt these three people had a soft spot in their hearts for me. They've been there for me when I needed companionship, laughs, deep conversations. But something happened to me last year. After my world fell apart and I spent a year deciding if I was going to keep living, I constructed new walls around my gear and my life and started letting things slowly past those doors. First, things that were necessary for life - aka food and water. Next, things that nourished me in the pain -

maybe that was first, like alcohol and TV. Then people who had been there for me throughout that time. I was testing the waters. And when I got to those three, the interactions were triggering and painful. But the new me is over that bullshit. So two, I told how it impacted me, and one, I stopped replying because they couldn't handle the truth. And from each of them I got back, "but I love you." Take my pitiful, self-centered behavior again because I love me. I mean, you. I love you. When I'm not feeling as strong, I can understand all the factors in their lives that make them only see life through their lenses. I am an understanding and considerate person who is able to see situations from multiple viewpoints. And I almost forgive them because I am not one to cut off relationships. And if they die, I don't want any regrets. And over time, I forget the pain they re-inflicted a couple months previously. So I reach back out, or reply to their text about nothing, acknowledging nothing, testing the waters. And within seconds, my reply is met with the truth of their character, and I am injured anew. And I can't tell if I'm a bear caught in a trap who still thinks he's free or if I've just been stung by bees, and I can run away and dunk in the water to wash it all off. My former definitions of how I am a good person don't serve me in my new life. I believed being selfless was the ultimate example of love. But that led me to collect a group of family and friends who cannot express self-less love to me for an extended period of time, who do not have the introspection necessary to examine their behavior and call it what it is, who wants me to say, sure, keep being an ass and I'll take it. Those days are over. Stop hurting me. That is not love.

June 2019

I need to decide what my relationship with _____ is going to be. We keep arguing, and I'm over it. She refuses to see my point of view on my grief and she makes this about her, and I simply don't have the time. I've purposefully not told her or _____ about my job. I know how judgmental they are about work and intelligence and success, and I didn't want to deal with that. But since work and recover (aka sleep) is all I do, it's made it hard to catch up with people. And I haven't been talking to my family as much. It's sad and triggering because it reminds me of my loss, and it takes me a week and a lot of drinking to recover emotionally. But I keep doing it because I wish I kept in touch more. So we have that cycle - talk to them, feel discomfort, get pushed to the edge, hurt, grief spiral, retreat, recover, time passes, think about wanting no regrets, more time, no regrets, call, regret. So anyway, I figured if I was ever going to talk to _____ again, I'd eventually have to tell her about my entry-level job. I decided to call from the airport after an amazing girls' weekend, time constraints because of the impending flight; already in a good mood, and I had drink coupons for the flight ahead. So I call. And immediately get questions. Like, dude, I called you. You ain't call me to catch up. So let me drive the convo. But no, you're always in control. So fine. "I've been up to a great weekend. We did x, y, and z... rejuvenating...grew as women and wives." Her, "Oh. What else have you been up to?" Deep breath. "I started a part-time job, and I really like it." "Where?" Not, doing what,

61

or glad to hear you're getting out! Or that must have been such hard work for you. 'Cause, what matters is "where." "A coffee shop, and it's been great. I really like it." My thinking, let her know up front that I'm happy there, it's been great, so treat this like it's a good thing. My plan is to give her the info I gave in my interview as to why I have a Master's degree and over 10 years of experience in a career but am choosing to work minimum wage - I've always wanted to own a coffee shop by the beach and provide coffee and tapas for my customers. And working here helps me learn from the bottom up. I hope to work my way up through the company and learn about all the facets of running a coffee shop. Make it acceptable to her that I've made the best decision for my mental health. But what she does next shocks me. She laughs. An uncontrollable cackling-sounding laugh. I tell her I have a job that I like, and her response is to laugh. And say, "okaaaaay." I know I've been expecting judgy, so I don't want to jump to conclusions. Maybe she's picked up a PT job there too and is astonished at the coincidence. Maybe she's feeling self-righteous because she'd told me to work there before, but I didn't listen, and now I have no recollection that it was actually her idea in the first place?! So I ask calmly, straight, nice, "why are you laughing?" She says, "oh, nothing." So I repeat, I want to know, why are you laughing. She says, "because you are so smart and…" And I explode. Politely but firmly, "that's why I didn't want to tell you! You have no idea what I'm doing for them, why I'm doing it, all you know is who I work for and that I like it, and you've already decided it's not good enough!" Her: See, this is why I don't call you guys. I can never say anything! Me: So it's my fault you don't call and check on me? You hurt me every time I call you, yet I still do it. Well, not every time, but consistently [yes, I backtracked that in real time]. Her: You two are so secretive! Me: What?! I'm literally calling and updating you on what's going on in my life. Nothing has happened until now and I'm sharing it with you and your response was to laugh in my face. You need to change that narrative because you keep saying I'm secretive but I'm literally here trying to talk to you. I don't have any secrets! The only thing I said I don't want to talk about is my mom! Her: Well, I want to know how you guys are going! Me: "I'm trying to tell you, but all you want to talk about is my mom, and I've told you I can't do that right now. I don't want to talk about her every time I call you. I need to stay upbeat. If you need someone to talk about her with, talk to your therapist. I can't handle it." And on and on. And back to the job and me repeating that she doesn't even know anything about it. So, she finally asked what I do. And I realize I shouldn't have to make this about the future. I shouldn't have to justify why I need a transitional job. I shouldn't have to justify to someone who knows how depressed I was (yet seems determined to put me back in that state) why this job has been good for me. And I don't want to diminish the value the job has <u>right</u> <u>now</u>. It's not about my future aspirations. It's that this repetitive job, with the incredibly nice people, the challenging mental work of learning the drinks and machinery and register, and being forced to smile, and being relied upon each day to show up and do my best, and no one knowing my past or my pain - that's been great for me. And I don't feel like sharing my heart with her anymore. I'm sure she'd understand. But why do I have to force her to be willing to learn more before passing judgment? And continually reminding me that what she wants from me, I'm not giving. Why is my grieving process about how I can support her through her grief? And continue to let her judge me and my life? It's always been about proving my smarts and giving her something to brag about. I thought that was cool in the past, but now that I'm struggling, you don't want to share that, and I'm not giving you the bragging stories I used to. So I don't want to talk anymore. I told her I wasn't interested in talking about the job anymore. She fought, but I didn't budge. So she asked about the Warriors. We made small talk for a little bit. I wanted to get off the phone, but I didn't want to end with negativity, so I participated in the conversation. Then she brings up _____. Hard eye roll! Her: I haven't heard from him in a while. Me: *crickets*... "Okay, well, my flight is about to board." Forget it. She's like a child with a scab who only wants to discuss the cornerstone challenging things, which I understand. But I have told her <u>every time we talked</u> that I didn't want to discuss those 2 people! So now I'm left again wondering if she will not respect my boundaries. She is not respecting my process. She is not helping; in fact, she hurts me every damn time! She's a good person who goes above and beyond for the people she loves. She just wants me to do it her way, and it doesn't matter how much I try to teach her about how to approach sensitive topics (I literally told her to ask me how I'm doing [and you know I already outlawed that question, but I gave her special permission!] and if I'm able, I'll talk about the things I know she wants me to), she refuses to do things any other way than how she wants to, and then she gets mad at me. So I kinda don't want to talk to her anymore. Why would I? This cycle is dumb and draining. I'm over doing things because it makes other people feel better. I want the salve. I'm ready to feel better. But I don't. I'm not doing well, and these people and their forced painful "love" make me question if I'm the bad person, the selfish one, and I don't know the balance between appropriate consideration of self and selfishness. I'm sick of having these conversations trying to explain myself and figure out the other person, then things continuing on just as they've always been. It's exhausting and painful, and I think so much less of them afterward. And my sis wants to have that convo with ____ soon. I don't have it to give. But I'll support her. 'Cause that's love, bitches.

Date Unknown

I feel so icky, so tired, so peopled out, and on days like today, I wish I had disability to help provide for my family. I work so hard for pennies. I can't even imagine if I had to perform at the level I did before. Fuck! I want to call off but I don't want to lose my job. I need a day. Or a week. Or my life back. This sucks. I hate America. This country only values the rich. Fucks the poor. And makes it impossible to rise above your situation unless you have a father who can loan you $10 million. Or even $10K. Fuck!

July 2019

I just got home from a Kirk Franklin concert. I'm not sure if you're aware of who he is, but he is arguably the most influential gospel artist of all time. I say 'arguably' because my mom and my husband's dad argued (separately) that Walter Hawkins was the most influential, but Kirk took gospel music to a whole other level, made it cool, introduced it to people who weren't Christian, and he's been going for 27 years strong and counting. I'm also ready to argue that he is the most talented musician of our time. And I've seen Beyoncé (and would pay another of my PT minimum wage earned paychecks to see her again) and Michael Jackson (whose talent is indescribable). The way Kirk weaves songs together, envisions new chords out of the same ol' 13 notes everyone else has, combines words with those notes, and transports you to every emotion and experience possible is pure genius. He doesn't make you want to be him or have his riches and lifestyle; he makes you want to know his God as he does. To have a life-transforming relationship that anchors every horrible and beautiful experience and gives you confidence in a greater plan. And even though I didn't want to, I felt it. I don't know what that means, but I did feel it.

The challenge is that music is connected to the soul in a way that reality - or the reality of God - isn't. The emotions that stir and rumble and overflow when listening to Kirk's music and story are just chemical reactions to very powerful and genius-led inspiration. I truly want to feel how he does and to believe there is a master plan, but the unknown plan and accepted suffering that seem to have to be interwoven with faith are inexcusable for me. If He is responsible for the good, then He is responsible for the bad. And if you don't want to explain why a father and daughter lost their lives seeking shelter or a family was swept away in a flash flood, or a deranged man killed the mother of his children and also, if you don't understand how that all fits into the plan, then we are suffering in vain, without specific ways to grow, and the slave masters and corrupt people continue to use belief in God's master plan as a tool of hope to subdue the masses until they die so that their rule can be easier, unchallenged and endless. Yes, there will be bright stars like Kirk, and many lives will have shining moments of joy, but there are equally moments of inexplicable pain and suffering. How is that okay? How is that even acceptable? I also know that without faith in God, my husband wouldn't have made it through this last year with me, and I'm grateful his faith bolstered him and reinforced his strength when I couldn't and didn't want to.

April 13, 2020

We are currently in the time of COVID-19. And there are so many emotions about that that I don't have the energy to get into. But this time has allowed me to type up my book, and transfer the handwritten scribblings into the book I wanted them to become. It's been hard going back over these emotions and these thoughts. I can see progress has been made, and I can see how I'm still the same. I see where I was in such pain or in such a rush to get the words out that the words are barely formed, and I have to decipher my own writing, and in some places, I'm still not 100% sure what I said. But I tried.

Yesterday was our three-year anniversary! Wow. So much has happened in such a short amount of time. Anyway, today my job projected the calendar for the next 3 weeks. The last one said May 4-8: Teacher Appreciation Week and May 10: Mother's Day. For real? How in the heck did that come again so quickly? It's crazy how many days bring negative feelings for me. January - her birthday. March - my sister's birthday, and my mom can't sing her happy birthday or call at her time of birth, as was our tradition. April - my anniversary, and reminiscing and looking at pics just isn't possible yet without feeling deep sadness, yet I'm also so happy for our relationship. Plus, they start advertising for… May - Mother's Day, yuck. June - Father's Day and unwanted reminders. July - her death. How the hell do they expect me to handle that whole month? August/September - school year starts and I think of how she would have loved another year helping her students. October - I start stressing about the months to come. November - my favorite holiday, without my favorite. December - my birthday, the big family holiday of Christmas, being forced to reflect on the previous year and expected to make New Year's resolutions. Boo to all that shit. Right back to January. It hurts.

Final Journal Entry

I've reached a point where I'm unsure of the purpose of this book. There's self-help, personal story sharing, tips on supporting those who are grieving, life questions, some things helpful, some a complete downer. How to package this so someone else wants to read it? I wanted my story to matter, to help someone else. Did it? Did I? Or are you just more depressed now and in need of liquor? Oh, I'm sorry, is that just me?!

My Letter

I originally wrote a letter to my father in this book. A way to memorialize what happened in the immediate years after my mother's passing. I've decided to remove it. It's too personal, and it doesn't feel right to include it. Plus, I don't want this book to be used as an instrument of pain.

Suffice it to say; that was Major Loss #3.

What I think is helpful to share is that every person deals with grief differently. And not everyone can be there for you in those moments and in all the ones that follow. Boundaries need to be created and re-examined as you continue on. I hope you don't lose relationships as I have. But if you feel it necessary to move on, I hope you have the courage and means to do so.

Well, look at me, believing in hope after all.

Acknowledgments

I had to decide how much I wanted outside forces to influence my book. It was hard because I think it was critical for my survival that I had outside sources of information to help me through hell. Yet, concurrently, I didn't want others to feel as though I had copied their work, so a balance had to be struck. I happily credit those who influenced me, and I hope you read their work as well. I am heavy on the first-person narrative, so you will know what my experience is and what my thoughts are. My goal is not to explain others' work, so I don't believe I can have misrepresented them; I only put forth what I took from reading their perspectives.

"When Bad Things Happen to Good People" by Harold S. Kushner. This was the first book I read related to the loss. This nonfiction book gave me language for the swirl of feelings - nay conclusions - I had reached for why God does not exist. It is important to note that this is not the author's conclusion or message.

When I first heard the title of this book, I just knew it would be about "there are no good people, so bad things aren't undeserved." I've heard those sermons before when pastors tried to explain the answer to that question. And when I flipped through the first few pages, I was shocked to discover it had been written by a rabbi and would be discussing God. Since the book had been recommended in session 1 by my then-therapist in a secular (non-church) environment, whom I believe I had already told that I did not believe in God, I assumed she would not recommend a religious book (can you hear my eye roll?). But there we were; I decided to read it because I was floundering, and it had a strong intro. About 30 pages in, I ended up starting the book over, but this time, with a yellow highlighter, an orange pen for underlining, and pink Post-Its to flag pages. About halfway through, I was simultaneously reading and figuring out whom I could ask to read it too because I knew I would need to discuss these concepts with someone intelligent, with similar religious beliefs as me (at least pre-loss), and who would be willing to read a book and upon request. Thank goodness I've got a sister just like that.

So, my 2nd acknowledgment is to her, my sister friend Jessica. For immediately agreeing to read the book, for agreeing that it needed to be discussed in person, and then her suggestion that she drive four hours to meet me where I would be for a couple of days with my husband for his business trip. If you don't have a friend in your life who would do that for you, get to searching. Join a book club, take some dance classes, and do something to meet people. She gave me a safe space and her unmatched combo of personal experience with our religion and its intersection with real life, her genius-level processing and communication skills, and her infinite love for me. Because of grief, my mind had/has short circuits, so words and thoughts did not flow well, and being given time and space to verbalize, figure out how to verbalize, test, and re-test while she did the same and appropriately challenged our theories, all helped me formulate what my remaining questions were and determine what concepts were swirling in me.

After three tragic and failed attempts at therapy where I left feeling worse about myself and life itself, which, who knew that was even possible, my next acknowledgment is to my grief therapist, who chose to become an expert in what has to be the most depressing, challenging work (except for maybe working with children who have been abused, though sadly, from my experience working with them, they showed more resilience than I did, which I don't even know how to deal with right now). So, uh, back to Dr. Z (as I affectionately call you to my husband)/Queen Z (as I also call you because you are amazing). She led me to a spot in hell where I could see blue skies and sunshine. And she gave me validation, language, and understanding right where I was. And she told me that the place we were looking at was not the same as the world I'd left, but it wasn't as bad as the hell I was currently living in. And she showed me how to build a bridge between my old world and my new one. And she did all that in just two sessions. Dr. Z, I hope you don't hate this acknowledgment because I cannot say enough about how you saved my life.

My husband asked me why the validation helps so much. Going through this, you truly feel crazy. There are gaps in your memory. You are a very different person than you were before. Time stops making sense. There is a physical sense of not being attached to the ground at times. You are physically and emotionally experiencing things that people—sometimes including professionals—tell you are not real, though you actually are experiencing them. You've read or seen things that are contrary to what you're actually going through (e.g., the 5 stages of grief, movies with death in them, previously-attended funerals, church teachings, own belief systems), so you think you should be acting/feeling/thinking differently. Plus, add in that you aren't sleeping, or if you are, it doesn't feel restful, and remember that sleep deprivation is a form of actual torture for a reason...yeah, validation is extremely helpful. It's grounding at the moment. You can finally believe yourself and your experience. For me, the validation usually came with an explanation or additional language of some sort, which was also helpful at a time when I was at a loss for words as a person who was historically adept with words.

Thank you to the friends and family who kept reaching out to me, who endured times when I lashed out, who hopefully had group chats behind my back to say what they needed to say about me and get themselves readied for battle with my complicated ass, who gave me moments of happiness and moments where I was able to get out of my head and participate in real life, who are still patient with me now, and who are allowing our relationships to evolve. I hope I can be a good friend to you again in my new reality.

My final 2 acknowledgments are much more difficult to write. The depth to which they have lived this with me and helped me through it cannot be expressed, but they know it.

Lil Girl, you are the part of me that lives outside my body. You helped keep our mother alive. You convinced me to find a therapist who is a grief expert. And you said the mean stuff to others when it needed to be said. I'm so sorry this tragedy has befallen on you too.

Love, you walked Every Single Day with a crazy-in-grief wife, who had hints of crazy before but who I'm sure you never could have expected all of this to come from! You chose to walk with me—and carry me at times—through hell while I kicked and screamed and cursed. You kept my heart beating. You kept our home running. And you did it with a genuine smile, continual kindness and respect, and with humor. And we discovered that the only imitation he's good at is Elmo!

And that's that.

NOTES

_____

_____

_____

_____

_____

_____

_____

_____

_____

_____

_____

_____

_____

_____

_____

_____

_____

_____

_____

_____

_____

_____

_____

Notes

WRITING RELEASES, THE THOUGHTS THAT BUILD UP INSIDE OF YOU

Notes

_____
_____
_____
_____
_____
_____
_____
_____
_____
_____
_____
_____
_____
_____
_____
_____
_____
_____
_____
_____
_____
_____
_____
_____
_____
_____
_____

FIND YOUR VILLAGE. FIND THOSE WHO WILL POUR INTO YOU

IF YOU WISH TO MOVE MOUNTAINS, START BY LIFTING STONES TODAY.

_____
_____
_____
_____
_____
_____
_____
_____
_____
_____
_____
_____
_____
_____
_____
_____
_____
_____
_____
_____
_____
_____

EMBRACE YOUR THOUGHTS AND FEELINGS

_____
_____
_____
_____
_____
_____
_____
_____
_____
_____
_____
_____
_____
_____
_____
_____
_____
_____
_____
_____
_____
_____
_____
_____
_____
_____
_____

SOMETIMES, YOU JUST NEED TO VENT

IF YOU'RE READING THIS, YOU ARE AMAZING.

Notes

YOUR EXPERIENCE IS VALID.

AFTER WAR, COMES PEACE

_____

_____

_____

_____

_____

_____

_____

_____

_____

_____

_____

_____

_____

_____

_____

_____

_____

_____

_____

_____

_____

_____

_____

_____

_____

_____

WHAT ELSE DO YOU NEED TO TALK ABOUT?

www.ingramcontent.com/pod-product-compliance
Lightning Source LLC
Chambersburg PA
CBHW060336130626
46553CB00003B/1011